Guess Who We

Mary Garcia
Illustrated by Gaston Vanzet

We walk to school every day.

Mr. Petrov is the crossing guard.

He helps us cross the street.

"Thanks, Mr. Petrov," we say.

On Monday, Mr. Petrov stopped a builder's truck.

"I would like to be a builder," said Carlos.
"I would build houses."

On Tuesday, Mr. Petrov stopped a mail truck.

"I would like to be a letter carrier," said Talia.
"I would deliver people's mail."

On Wednesday, Mr. Petrov stopped a plumber's van.

"I would like to be a plumber," said Eddie.
"I would fix people's sinks."

On Thursday, Mr. Petrov stopped a gardener's truck.

"I would like to be a gardener," said Yuki.
"I would take care of the park."

On Friday, Mr. Petrov stopped a police car.

"I would like to be a police officer," said Emma.
"I would make sure people are safe."

On Saturday, we did not go to school.
We walked to the fair.

Can you guess who we saw?

"Hi," said Mr. Petrov.

"I like being a crossing guard and a clown!"